# I AM

## 40-DAY DEVOTIONAL FOR SINGLES

## Discovering God When Life Doesn't Go As Planned

## Dionnea Seals

Gabuchi Publishing House
CHICAGO, IL

All Scripture quotations, unless otherwise indicated, are taken from the Holy Bible, New International Version®, NIV®. Copyright ©1973, 1978, 1984, 2011 by Biblica, Inc.™ Used by permission of Zondervan. All rights reserved worldwide. www.zondervan.com The "NIV" and "New International Version" are trademarks registered in the United States Patent and Trademark Office by Biblica, Inc.™

Scriptures marked ESV are taken from the THE HOLY BIBLE, ENGLISH STANDARD VERSION (ESV): Scriptures taken from THE HOLY BIBLE, ENGLISH STANDARD VERSION ®Copyright© 2001 by Crossway, a publishing ministry of Good News Publishers. Used by permission.

Scriptures marked NLT are taken from the HOLY BIBLE, NEW LIVING TRANSLATION
(NLT): Scriptures taken from the HOLY BIBLE, NEW LIVING TRANSLATION, Copyright©
1996, 2004, 2007 by Tyndale House Foundation. Used by permission of Tyndale House Publishers, Inc., Carol Stream, Illinois 60188. All rights reserved. Used by permission.

Scriptures marked NKJV are taken from the NEW KING JAMES VERSION (NKJV): Scripture
taken from the NEW KING JAMES VERSION®. Copyright© 1982 by Thomas Nelson, Inc.
Used by permission. All rights reserved.

Scripture quotations marked (GNT) are from the Good News Translation in Today's English Version- Second Edition Copyright © 1992 by American Bible Society. Used by Permission.

**I AM: Discovering God When Life Goes Unplanned, 40-Day Devotional For Singles**
**Copyright © 2017 by Dionnea Seals**

All rights reserved. No part of this publication may be reproduced, distributed, or transmitted in any form or by any means, including photocopying, recording, or other electronic or mechanical methods, without the prior written permission of the publisher, except in the case of brief quotations embodied in critical reviews and certain other noncommercial uses permitted by copyright law. For permission requests, write to the publisher, addressed "Attention: Permissions Coordinator," at the address below.

Dionnea Seals/Gabuchi Publishing House
Chicago, Illinois/60643
www.a-single-moment.com

I AM/ Dionnea Seals —1st ed.
ISBN Print 978-0-9988670-0-7
ISBN Ebook 978-0-9988670-1-4

# Contents

Introduction ............................................. 1
Your Living Water ................................. 11
Your Faithful God ................................. 17
Your Sustainer ...................................... 23
Your Promise Keeper ........................... 29
Your Solid Rock .................................... 37
Your Protector ...................................... 43
Your Friend ........................................... 51
Your King .............................................. 57
Your Father ........................................... 63
Your Defender ...................................... 69
Your Redeemer ..................................... 75
Your Savior ........................................... 81
Your Joy ................................................ 87
Your Light ............................................. 93
Your Hero ............................................. 99
Your Shield ......................................... 105
Your Love ............................................ 111

| | |
|---|---|
| Your Reward | 117 |
| Your Heart Keeper | 123 |
| Your Potter | 129 |
| Your Healer | 135 |
| Your Strength | 141 |
| Your Restorer | 147 |
| Your Answer | 153 |
| Your Advocate | 159 |
| Your Creator | 165 |
| Your Portion | 171 |
| Your Comfort | 177 |
| Your Peace | 183 |
| Your Shepherd | 189 |
| Your Load Bearer | 195 |
| Your Rest | 201 |
| Your Provider | 207 |
| Your Grace | 213 |
| Your Hope | 219 |
| Your Source | 225 |
| Your Deliverer | 231 |
| Your Way of Escape | 237 |
| Your Living Word | 243 |
| Your Everything | 249 |

## Dedication

To the greatest love of my life, JESUS CHRIST. Without you, I cease to be. I love you more and more each day. Thank you Lord for giving me this assignment for such a time as this.

To my parents: Robert and Teresa Seals

To my sister: Landria Seals Green

To all singles who find themselves frustrated with their journey. I've been there and I prayerfully stand with you. Be encouraged and know that your season will change. God is faithful.

*Jeremiah 29:11-13, "For I know the plans I have for you, says the Lord. They are plans for good and not for disaster, to give you a future and a hope. In those days when you pray, I will listen. If you look for me wholeheartedly, you will find me."*

## ACKNOWLEDGMENTS

To my parents, thank you for your unwavering love, prayers, and support. You are such a great example of putting God first in marriage and family. I am forever grateful that you belong to me.

To my sister, Landria Seals Green, who always encourages me to take the leap and gives me great ideas. Your influence continues to shape the woman I become.

To Diane Jackson, who over the years, patiently listened to my rants about being single. Thank you for your prayers, encouragement, and telling me to write down all that I was learning.

To Kimberly Jones Franklin, my friend and confidant who keeps me focused. Thank you for your support with so many things over the years.

To Pam, thank you for your friendship, prayer, and great chats about the Lord.

To Sharon Honeywood, whose statement 'next in line', continues to remind me to write my books.

To SNS Edits, thank you for helping me develop as an author.

# INTRODUCTION

"God, I feel duped." Duped. Also known as deceived and tricked. Yes, those were the actual words I said to Him as I struggled to grasp and accept my current circumstances. I laugh now, especially at my choice of words, but it was no laughing matter back then. Thirty-six years old, single, and *still* waiting on God to deliver His promise. I'd had my moments of calm and contentment, but lately it had gotten out of hand. Perhaps celebrating news of recent engagements and marriages began my emotional upheaval. God appeared to certainly be in the neighborhood with others, He just wasn't on *my* block ... yet. With one eyebrow raised to heaven, my question of 'how long' turned into, you've got to be kidding me! I began to grow weary during the time in-between the promise of marriage and the manifestation.

My age growing closer to forty, I had been waiting quite a while for His promise: marriage. From a young age, I knew the gift of singleness was not given to me. Not only did I have the desire for marriage, but promises made from Him and confirmations clued me in that marriage was a gift He had in store. Not only was I waiting for that, but during the midst of *this* particular time, some unexpected life changes came without warning and, needless to say, without my permission. My life had a to-do list and I was the last one to know. It was all overwhelming. Like a domino effect, the chips kept falling even as I tried hard to keep it together. Questionable health, beginning a doctoral program, job, and relationship transitions all competed for my attention. However, rejecting the lies of the enemy proved to be the most challenging issue I faced.

What I didn't realize at the time was that God was more interested in transforming me through my circumstances, while I was still waiting on Him to fulfill His promise.

Recently, at the age of 37, I surveyed the past twelve years and finally agreed with God: His timing is definitely better than my own. Throughout my season of waiting, a new level of trust and contentment found its way in, as I made the choice to savor all that life was offering. However, leaving frustration behind and moving to freedom did not happen overnight.

Maybe God is calling you deeper as He has been calling me, "Come closer and get to know me more. Look at the times in your life where I led you and held you."

We know God as a Promise Keeper. We know Him as Love. But what happens when the promise seems out of reach? What happens when the vision takes longer to come to pass than we think it should? While we're waiting for our appointed time, life continues to unfold. If we're honest with ourselves, as much as we love Him, frustration and questions of doubt find their way into our minds. Sometimes it's hard to share emotions with those closest to us. We've all been there before. Family or friends with preconceived notions and automatic thinking, blindly assuming that all is well when that couldn't be further from the truth.

At times, the difficulty lies in maintaining our walk with Him as curve balls are thrown our way. When you've done *most* things right, yet life fails to respond the way *we* think is best, questioning God with a list of why's most often come before the acceptance of yes to His plan.

Growing up, I always enjoyed and related to the story of Joseph. Not because of the jealousy and betrayal from members of his family, but because the promise shown to him of things to come at an early age was similar to my own. Joseph was single and encountered many detours on the road to destiny. From jealousy to injustice, his journey led him to fulfill the promise of God for his life and the saving of others.

God was not blind to all that happened to Joseph. God may not have authored it, but He allowed Joseph to experience trials that did not deviate from God's ultimate and intended plan for his life.

During the course of his journey, Joseph was falsely accused and thrown into jail. God could have gotten him out sooner rather than later. However, God chose to keep Joseph in a place where he could rehash or reflect on all that had occurred. Joseph had to be ready for the promise and his place of destiny had to be ready for Joseph. In other words, his time-out experience proved to be just what he needed, adding to the wonderful picture he could yet to see.

Singles, I believe our season can also be viewed as a time out. It's in this middle time that we gauge our attitudes in response to predicaments. The choice to believe when all is silent. A moment to decide *if* we'll believe and decide to keep trusting when all the doors are shut. The middle is the making and breaking point of our attitudes, beliefs, and assumptions. Where we're challenged to fight, stand, and get to the other side of wait.

Just like Joseph, God has given us an opportunity to reflect on our journey and get excited about what's to come. I'll admit that a lot of my time could have been more usefully and carefully spent. The opportunity to know God deeper and on new levels can be what propels us to gain more tools before we get to the promise.

At the end of the day, no matter if God has promised marriage to some or to all, the capacity to know Him in so many ways will be on each individual. Perhaps God is wondering, "Do they even want to get to know me, or are they content in knowing what I can do for them? Do you only want the promise or do you want to get to know me, the Promise Keeper?"

Studying the life of Joseph in Genesis we find that God gave him several visions of his future. Joseph would in fact rule many, including his family. But God did not show him all that would happen to arrive as second in command. Perhaps showing him the middle would scare Joseph or cause him to have unbelief. Let's face it: the middle is messy. It's a place where dreams may die or become refined. A moment when relationships, romantic or otherwise, that once sustained you come to a screeching halt. A time when a report from the doctor forces you to question your own mortality.

We experience death of relationships (physically or emotionally), or sickness. What I've discovered is the middle does all of the above in preparation for your new beginnings. But to get to those new beginnings, we must go through the middle. I repeat, we must go through ... and come out the other side.

Recently I was asked where I got the idea for this devotional. Like you, I was at a point where I needed a word from God. I needed support and encouragement. Despite my best efforts, going to family and friends did not provide me with the missing link. I needed *something*. The Holy Spirit speaks a lot to me as I drive, impressing upon my heart revelations and ideas. One day while driving to work, the words I AM washed over me quickly and stopped my temptation to mentally go down 'pity party lane.' At that moment, God was giving me what I was looking for.

Those two words began to challenge me in thinking about who God was in my life, and who He'd been to me in my journey. As I began to think about God's faithfulness to me, one attribute of God had become many. The Holy Spirit kept pushing me to go deeper and before I knew it, my list had grown to forty.

God doesn't want us to settle for a surface relationship with Him. He desires for us to go deeper into knowing Him and His ways. By doing so, we find out more about ourselves, our purpose, and our inheritance in Christ. Taking my eyes off my circumstances and meditating on Him gave me the relief I so desperately needed. God ministered to me and gently reminded me of who He was and is. Maybe you've found yourself frustrated and stagnant in this journey.

Waiting on God for His promises to come to pass is not an easy task. With so many things going on, we can become tempted to believe our problems are out of control. To believe that God, who has the world in His hands, is not aware of our situation. That kind of thinking is a lie from the enemy. God wanted me to know how much He cares about me. Truly. Madly. Deeply. And He feels the same about you. Sit with Him and allow God to fill you with all that He is. What I'm discovering is that loneliness is a beckon for us to press into God.

From the temptation of Jesus to prophetic warnings and fasting from other great men in the Bible, the number forty is mentioned 146 times in the word of God. The number 40 symbolizes a moment to pause, to meditate on God and His plan for your life. This devotional will give you just enough time to rekindle and reflect on your relationship with God as you grow forward in His plan. As you carefully meditate during this time, opportunity to record your thoughts or promptings from the Holy Spirit is provided.

Sometimes we need to take the time to reflect on who He is, what He means to us, and what He's doing for us. This list of forty is just the beginning, because He's so much more. May you find your strength renewed and your faith filled to capacity to keep answering His call. May you continue on the road of becoming more like Him. There will be no greater love than the love that Jesus provides. As you continue to say yes to Him, married or not, keep your hands, heart, and mind open to His leading. No matter how long the wait for His plan, trust that God is sovereign. He hasn't forgotten about you, and He loves you dearly.

This gift of waiting, I discovered, can only be appreciated in the middle. In the life of Joseph, only God knows why He did not reveal the time in-between. All throughout his story, we see the words, "But the Lord was with Joseph." God's presence was with him in every turn and event of his life. Even as he sat in prison for ten years, waiting to be remembered and released, the Lord was with Joseph. And the same goes for us. Life doesn't stop while we wait on God, nor are we exempt from trials that cause us to question if He's there.

Our own prison may come in many shapes and sizes, beyond our control, or frame of time. But rest assured, God is with us. Joseph experienced many circumstances that could have caused him to abandon God, to let go of His promises, and to cling to unforgiveness. But as he sat in jail, I imagine the moments where quiet conversations with God turned into worship. When he had no words, Joseph's heart cried out and he reflected about what got him to that place. Yet, he did not forget about the promise. He may not have known how, but he knew Who. And that was most important.

As we sit in His waiting room, we have ample opportunity to dig deeper and get to know our Father. And actually, He's inviting us to do so. For no season in God is to be wasted. Our current time is no accident by God. If all things work together for good as the Bible says in Romans 8:28, then this is certainly a part of that good. Some may have experienced Him from a distance, yet others may know Him up close and personal. No matter where you are, we all need a reminder of who *He* is: I AM. Two words that are filled with so much truth and hope that has no ending.

Many introduce themselves by their occupation, gender, or marital status. Yet with Christ, we know Him simply as I AM. In Exodus 3:13-14, Moses asks God, "What should I tell them when they asked who sent me?" God's response? I AM WHO I AM. God made this distinction because of the many gods the Egyptians worshiped. But the One and True living God (I AM) was the same God who true believers worshipped hundreds of years earlier. I AM was the One whom they talked about and relied on. I AM was the One who came through on His promises. I AM was and still is, the One whose character had not and does not change.

I AM is the One who makes life complete.
Journey with me as we get to know our Lord and Savior Jesus Christ in this season, orchestrated by Him.
He is ... I AM.

DAY 1

# Your Living Water

*I am the bread of life. Whoever comes to me will never be hungry again. Whoever believes in me will never be thirsty.*

John 6:35

Thirsty. A common term meant to describe one's feeling to drink something. At least that's what I've known it to be growing up. However, these days, it takes on an entirely different meaning. Mention that word today and many would come up with descriptions of being too eager to get something, or feelings of desperation. There's a reason why we're told not to shop for food when we're hungry—we end up getting things that we shouldn't, only to satisfy the deep hunger or thirst within. Years can go by without a date or someone to call our own. As life throws many things at us, we can look at this area and decide to help God out. Perhaps having *this* can make me feel better about *that*. We search to fill a void and time after time we find out what may have filled that longing, still leave us wanting more. And so we begin searching again, for status, relationships, and success- until we come to a place knowing it is He who can fill the spot that was only reserved for Him.

The Samaritan woman met Jesus in the midst of her thirst (John 4). On that day, she came to get water from the well. Little did she know, she would meet Jesus who would give her a Spiritual solution to her private problem. Her sinful life and numerous men did not satisfy the deepest need she longed for- being filled with the Living Water, Jesus.

The invitation for relationship and salvation was extended to her on that day. Just like her, we're given the same opportunity to satisfy our thirst with Him.

If we take the time and get to know Him in our singleness, our relationships can be stronger and our purpose more intentional. The essential key of being ready for God's promises is discovering the Promise Keeper.

It's no coincidence that the human body cannot survive for more than three days without water. It is our sustainer and life support. This Bible verse not only gives us an analogy of our need for Him, but God gives us the prescription of our thirst.

If there was ever a need for more in life, He would be just that. He is the only One who can satisfy and quench our thirst. He is the One who promises to satisfy us with His water. He is the well that never runs dry.

*Prayer*

*Dear Lord, Thank you for being my living water. Without you, life wouldn't make sense. Please forgive me in thinking I can be filled with someone or something besides you. You are the one who can satisfy my deepest longings. Thank you for your continuous refreshing, always available to pour into my life. Amen.*

# DAY ONE REFLECTIONS

## DAY ONE REFLECTIONS

DAY 2

# Your Faithful God

*Jesus Christ is the same yesterday, today, and forever.*

Hebrews 13:8

Great expectations. We all have them. "I thought he/she loved me," or "I thought they were my friends." Relationships can give us emotional highs or lows, and have the capacity to make us better or bitter. I didn't want to believe I was being played like a yo-yo. However, years of being in a relationship where feelings were questioned and confusion was always present took its toll. At the end, my fragmented heart proved difficult to put back together as God walked me through years of healing. Amazing how rose-colored glasses become so clear when you get out of a situation or toxic relationship. Clinging tightly to words of promise from a flawed human will always set you up to fall below your desired outcome. All relationships will disappoint, because we're all flawed. Promises we intend to keep most often fall through.

So many times we find ourselves facing disappointment from others. Whether it's friends, family, or love relationships, our world can turn upside down when others disappoint, causing us to question whether God will stay true to His Word. As loving as they are, they will never be able to keep their word all the time.

But God is not like us. He doesn't change, and all of His promises are yes and amen. We can rest in the knowledge that God will never leave nor forsake us. Ever. He is consistent about His ways, His love, and His plan for your life. Transitions and change are bound to happen in our lives.

However, we can rest assured that no matter the trajectory of our sails, the Word of God will remain and He will never deviate from His Word. Why? Because He is the Word and He does not change. Faithful is our God!

## Prayer

*Dear Lord, thank you for being so faithful to me. Thank you for being the One I can always depend on. You've never failed or disappointed me. No matter what goes on in my life, I can trust that your faithfulness will always meet me there. You are the only One I can count on. Please help me to always be mindful of just how faithful you have been and will continue to be. Amen.*

## DAY TWO REFLECTIONS

## DAY TWO REFLECTIONS

DAY 3

# Your Sustainer

*And he is before all things, and in him all things hold together.*

Colossians 1:17, ESV

For twelve long years, she suffered. Trying many doctors along the way in hopes of a cure, there was no solution. Ostracized, rejected, and embarrassed, she could not live the life she desired. An unnamed woman in the Bible only known as the woman with the issue of blood became most known by the move of faith she made after twelve long years. Physically and emotionally exhausted, this woman's life was preserved by God even though her physical health was compromised. Hearing that Jesus was passing by, her need to be healed by the only One who could help prompted her to act.

Many of us have grown to place emphasis on the ending of her story. However, there is much to be said about the middle. In fact, there's a lot to be learned from the middle lives of those whose endings have been popularized. It's only in the middle that things are rearranged while death and growth of perspective and direction occurs. I could not have imagined that waiting on God for His chosen person and season to arrive would be more than ten years.

From the outside, no one would have guessed the emotional rollercoaster I sometimes found myself on. From the age of twenty-five, my desire to end this season and relieve the emotional suffering that singleness brought at times seemed to persist. What I once questioned in amazement concerning the physical ache of loneliness heard in others unfortunately became familiar to me. However, like the woman with the issue of blood, He sustained me during those times of uncertainty.

When I believed I could not hang on to my faith in Him, God breathed new life and purpose in me to carry on. When tempted to go outside of God's will and help Him accomplish His plan, I found my strength depleted. God may not relieve our burdens or sufferings when we desire. Yet, He will give us the capacity to keep going until our season of new beginnings.

And He can do the same for you. Months or years may go by, during which God is strengthening and pruning us, so that we can bear more fruit of patience and trust in Him for the ending He has in store. His sustaining power we gain as singles will be moments of reflection used to help others and conquer new territory in life.

## Prayer

*Dear Lord, thank you for your keeping power. You have sustained me during the midst of my suffering and unwanted moments. When I wanted to give up, you gave me the will and power to continue believing. I know your plan for my life will unfold. Please continue to strengthen me in mind, body, and spirit as I wait on you to bring me into my new season. Amen.*

## DAY THREE REFLECTIONS

## DAY THREE REFLECTIONS

DAY 4

# Your Promise Keeper

*God is not a man, so he does not lie. He is not human, so he does not change his mind. Has he ever spoken and failed to act? Has he ever promised and not carried it through?*

Numbers 23:19

When the days or years go by and the night gets dark, weariness often sets in. During those moments of vulnerability, it's easy to question whether His promises will come to past. The wait seems long and for some, it may be longer than hoped and desired. But God has His reasons and He has a plan. If anyone in the Bible could attest to knowing God as a promise keeper, it would be Abraham and Sarah. God promised Abraham a son years before the promise manifested. Throughout Abraham's story in Genesis, God repeatedly confirms His promise to him. Yet God did not reveal when the promise would come forth. I imagine that if Abraham and Sarah knew the details, they probably would have elected to forgo it. The number of years alone waiting on the manifestation, would make anyone rethink God's promise. The bible doesn't provide us with the details of their emotional journey, however, we can draw the conclusion that their experience was filled with some doubt, frustration, and unanswered questions- before, during, *and* after the birth of Isaac (Genesis 15-22). In addition, they teach us about the consequence when impatience takes the drivers' seat.

To this day, tension in the middle east rose out of the birth of Ishmael because they neglected to wait on God's timing. Abraham and Sarah waited twenty-five years for their promised son, Isaac. *Twenty-five years* of holding onto God's promise. Why did God make them wait that long?

You may be asking that very same question for yourself: *Lord, why am I still waiting*? And to be honest, it doesn't seem quite fair that you would have to wait longer than some. But there's a reason. With God, there's always a reason. In His infinite wisdom, He is too wise to make a mistake. God is not in the business of serving up half-baked promises or blessing us at the wrong time.

Many factors both seen and unseen come into play when God is at work. Because His ultimate will includes the transformational process of making YOU more like HIM, He is using this time to refine you. If you let Him. No other person can make a promise, no matter the length of time, and exceed what you thought would happen. That's the kind of God we serve. He'll never go back on His word. We can trust Him to make good on His promises, because that's a part of His divine character. God gives to some the gift of marriage, and to others the gift of singleness (1 Corinthians 7:7).

Both marriage and a call to singleness is equal in God's sight. If you don't know what God has called you to, simply ask Him. Whether marriage is your desire or not, God will NEVER forget what He's promised to do in your life. He will make it happen.

## Prayer

*Dear Lord, thank you for keeping your promise to me. At times, I get weary while waiting for your blessings to manifest in my life. But I know you are not man and that you would not lie. Please help me to keep my eyes focused on you no matter how long the wait. You will bring forth your promise when the time is right in my life. Please help me to trust you in the wait. You are faithful and true. Thank you in advance for the promise. Amen.*

## DAY FOUR REFLECTIONS

## DAY FOUR REFLECTIONS

DAY 5

# Your Solid Rock

*Trust in the Lord forever, for in God the Lord, we have an everlasting Rock.*

Isaiah 26:4

Life has a way of shaking us to our core. Without warning or reason, we can be rocked and swayed by events or news. A bad economy, unstable employment, and relationships that have abruptly ended can leave us questioning if we'd ever find sure footing again. So many times we go about our day to day, not realizing that as bad as it is, it hasn't gone *that* bad. Yes, it's rough and difficult to imagine that what was once comfortable has ended. The book of Job written in the Bible gives us a sober reminder that any given moment can take our breath away. In one day, Job lost his children, servants, and means of income. Sure enough, he was rocked by all that happen. Falling to his knees, Job responded by giving praise to God as he said, "The Lord gave and the Lord has taken away" (Job 1:21 NIV). With a statement like that, you would believe that Job's pain and hurt was diminished. That could not be further from the truth. Likewise, your emotional response to tragedy does not mean you are less than spiritual.

However, Job shows us how to respond when we face circumstances less than desired. Job's relationship with God laid the foundation for him to continue worshipping the One he leaned on. Though his world was shaken, Job's faith stood firm. His solid belief and knowing who God was gave him the ability to keep standing on the truest foundation he would ever know.

Perhaps you've experienced similar setbacks and obstacles that threaten to dismantle your faith. Though Job wasn't aware of what was coming, God knew. Through all your troubles, your faith and worship can show the world that God is your solid rock among all sinking sand.

## Prayer

*Dear Lord, thank you for being my solid rock. When my world is falling a apart and the future looks bleak, you remind me that my foundation is set on you. You give me the strength to stand and keep moving when I'd rather run and hide. It's because of your love, and knowing that you're never shaken nor surprised, that I continue to worship in the midst of the storm. Let my life bring glory to you always. Amen.*

# DAY FIVE REFLECTIONS

## DAY FIVE REFLECTIONS

DAY 6

# Your Protector

*Whoever dwells in the shelter of the Most High will rest in the shadow of the Almighty. I will say of the Lord, "He is my refuge and my fortress, my God in whom I trust." Surely he will save you from the fowler's snare and from the deadly pestilence. He will cover you with his feathers, and under his wings you will find refuge;*

Psalm 91:1-4

"If I knew then what I know now" are words often repeated to young adults from parents and loved ones. Ask any senior or great lifelong learner and they would agree that failing to heed warnings of places, situations, and relationships caused them to have regret. Break ups, closed doors, and His answer of "no" may leave us feeling rejected. The relationship that I wanted to be in was not the one God ordained. Not only was my error found in pursuit, but it was also found in stepping out of my role as a woman of God. Unlike popular advice according to the world, women were created to be found and pursued by men. Attempting to get someone's attention or coming off as assertive (calling first or asking him out on a date), can leave women open to vulnerability. Over the years, there were plenty of times when I believed asking to 'hang out' was innocent.

Although my intentions were pure, being the pursuer was never my God-given role. In addition, hanging onto false hope in the relationship with the smallest compliments and attention thrown my way also left me wide open to rejection. Looking back, I realize that one person's no can be interpreted as God's closed doors.

For years, pride kept me trying to open the door in this relationship that God had bolted shut. It can be daunting to see His "no" as being protection from things unseen. After some time had passed, that gentleman who I so wanted to be with resurfaced with sure signs of hope and change. However, this time I was skeptical and treaded very lightly. Lo and behold, a dream God gave to me one night indicated that choosing to go forth and even entertain the thought of rekindling the romance would be detrimental to my spiritual walk.

This dream was evidence of the protection God was giving me. God wanted to protect my heart from hurting more than it had to. As I heeded His warning, I knew that His protection would prove to be the emotional guard that I needed. And that's what He desires to do in the lives of believers.

God provides physical, spiritual, and emotional protection if we allow Him to do so. Whether we understand the reasoning behind His answer of no is irrelevant in the grand scheme of things. God can see around corners before we even dare to arrive. He can also assess the hearts of others and know who to embrace and who to avoid.

Obedience and accepting His will serves as another layer of the love and protection He has promised. Refuse to see the no's in life as less than. Rather, embrace the adage: rejection is God's protection, to help you move forth in all that He has in store.

## Prayer

*Dear Lord, thank you for protecting me from seen and unseen danger. Thank you for protecting my heart from suitors who are less than best and ideal for my life. I give you all of me to guide and protect. Help me to see and trust that your answer of 'no and wait' are protective measures for my heart. Until the time is right, I know that you will guide and release me to the best will for my life. Amen.*

## DAY SIX REFLECTIONS

## DAY SIX REFLECTIONS

DAY 7

# Your Friend

*One who has unreliable friends soon come to ruin, but there is a friend who sticks closer than a brother.*

Proverbs 18:24

It's so easy to assume those who are married do not experience loneliness. As singles, it's tempting to believe and expect that feelings of loneliness would end after saying "I do." That couldn't be further from the truth. Whether you're single by choice or married, moments come where individuals experience some form of loneliness. Like an unexpected wind, it comes out of nowhere, leaving behind questions of worth and assessments of your own likability factor. The truth is, we were created to be relational and not experience this life in isolation. Perhaps it's time to view loneliness with a different perspective. The call of our hearts to connect with another can be used as a sign to draw near to God. After all, He was the constant friend before others came onto scene. It's often said if you can count the number of your friends on one hand, then you're blessed. Holding friends too tightly can also prove to be a hindrance to our growth.

Unconsciously running to *them* for answers first, instead of seeking God. Yet for others, the ebb and flow of seasons has suddenly caused a shift. Finding difficulty in the occurrence of when and how things changed.

When seasons change in our lives, we don't expect friendships to change as well. Most often, the ending may seem abrupt and without blame from both parties. But as the tide changes, God may reveal the intent and purpose of that particular friendship.

Nevertheless, no matter who comes and goes, you must know that HE is the ultimate friend who will never leave your side no matter the seasons in your life. He desires to be the One you come running to. Use this time to cultivate a friendship with Christ that will be without ending.

Rest assured, God will provide you with those who He wants you connected with.

## Prayer

*Dear Lord, thank you for being my friend, and thank you for showing me how to be a friend. Please help me to seek you first, knowing that your friendship will always sustain and add value to my life. Help me to discern that any call to loneliness is a call to draw near to you. Thank you for calling me friend. Amen.*

## DAY SEVEN REFLECTIONS

## DAY SEVEN REFLECTIONS

DAY 8

# Your King

> *"I am the Alpha and Omega," says the Lord God, "who is, and who was, and who is to come, the Almighty."*
>
> Revelation 1:8

There's a story in the Old Testament where Israel begged for a king to lead them. They were so desperate to be like other nations, their request for a king burdened the prophet Samuel. Troubled by their demands, Samuel prayed to the Lord and was given this answer: "It is not you they have rejected, but they have rejected me as their king ... but warn them solemnly and let them know what the king who will reign over them will do" (1 Samuel 8:9). From God's description, the King would do more harm than good. Yet, Israel still wanted *this* specific desire. They've forgotten so quickly how God delivered and provided for them.

Israel did not understand that the relationship they had with God was unlike what other nations had.

Like them, there are times when we fail to realize our blessings. Similar to the children of Israel, we desire for our lives to be like those we love and admire. We can get seduced by pictures or words as others display new relationships, etc. on social media. The reality is that God knows exactly where you are. Not only your physical location, but your emotional and mental state as well.

Withholding fulfillment of your desire for marriage does not indicate an unwillingness to bless you. From the children of Israel, it is clear that believing 'something is better than nothing,' can be just as detrimental to your life and well-being as being single.

Allowing this season to train your eyes to see just how much God has already provided for you will impact your life and the lives of others. Through your patience and submission to God, others will see your needs being met by the Ultimate King.

## Prayer

*Dear Lord, Thank you for being my King. Thank you for taking care of me when I did not fully realize you were doing so. Forgive me for believing the lie that anything less would satisfy. I know you have an awesome plan that includes love in your timing. Please help me to keep my eyes on you and embrace all that you have already given to me. Amen.*

## DAY EIGHT REFLECTIONS

## DAY EIGHT REFLECTIONS

DAY 9

# Your Father

*Though my mother and father forsake me, the Lord will receive me.*

Psalm 27:10

Hearing the words "Daddy's girl" or "chip off the old block," we know right away the impact a father has made in someone's life. My roots stem from a family whose lineage of strong fathers goes back at least three generations. Stories of their strength, perseverance, and love was the norm as I grew up and created goals for my life. Blessed to receive the outpouring of affection and knowledge from my father has always been the springboard for my personal and professional growth. However, even great men come with flaws. No matter how great of an example one's parent can be, they will never be able to match the perfection of our Heavenly Father. All throughout the Bible, we see the patriarchal role and example that fathers can bring. Through blessings or curses, many families were defined by their fathers' role, wealth, and spiritual example. From biblical days to the present, the standards and rules have not changed. Whether your father was present or not in the home, emotional or physical rejection from him can cause deep pain. Many successful or failed romantic relationships have deep roots in familial upbringing, exposing the desire to emulate our fathers or marry someone *like* them.

No matter if your home was defined as broken or successful, the connector of knowing God as our Father can turn rejection into chosen, and broken into whole. God always has time to hear from His children and we're never far from His thoughts. Through His character, we get a glimpse of what a Father's love truly looks like. God's protection, love, and acceptance is trustworthy.

In Him, we have blessings and direction. When you remember who you belong to, you can rise above the pain of the past and soar as your Father intended. We have a Father who never fails, and longs to hold us in the palm of His hand.

## Prayer

*Dear Lord, thank you for being my Heavenly Father. Thank you for always choosing me and never rejecting me. You have held me and shown that your love cannot be compared to others. Your ways and thoughts toward me are higher than I could imagine. As I run into your arms, I know that I am fully kept and strengthened by your embrace. Please help me to continue seeing the beauty of your perfection and acceptance. Amen.*

## DAY NINE REFLECTIONS

## DAY NINE REFLECTIONS

DAY 10

# Your Defender

*The Lord is your mighty defender, perfect and just in all his ways; Your God is faithful and true; he does what is right and fair.*

Deuteronomy 32:4, GNT

Defense wins games. Being a sports enthusiast, I know that a great defensive team can prevent its opponent from scoring and causing the other to have the advantage. Likewise, many spend thousands on having the best defense in law. There's nothing better than when people can vouch for your great reputation and prove that you've done no wrong. When you're defended, security and assurance awaits—even when vindication takes longer than expected. In the Bible, Joseph found himself falsely accused of being with his boss's wife. As a result, he was thrown in jail with seemingly no hopes of getting out. Even as time passed, it is known that God was with Joseph (Genesis 40:21). Spending years in prison for false accusations did not hinder God's presence being with him. In God's orchestrated time and way, Joseph was released and given a position higher than before. He didn't have a lawyer to defend or bail him out while in prison. Yet, Joseph had God who repeatedly said "I am with you." Joseph's reputation was so outstanding, he even found favor with the prison guards.

When others are motivated to do wrong against you, God gives us clear instructions on how to handle them. His answers appear to be defeating, but His goal to win your case is always at hand. And, might I add, He *never* loses a case: *It is mine to avenge; I will repay. In due time, their foot will slip ... Deuteronomy 32:35.*

One of the hardest things to do is be silent when you'd rather prove your case or point. Taking a step in my own life by choosing to trust God rather than doubt His provision continues to teach me about God's defending power. False accusations and assumptions on the job led to one of the biggest lessons received. What could have been a teachable moment by administration quickly turned into what appeared to be a firing squad against me.

I could have shrunk under pressure as defeat threatened to overtake me. But I stood in courage, knowing the maltreatment experienced did not match the admonishment I received. In the midst of that trial, God displayed His promise to take care of me. While standing on faith and truth, being at peace with the outcome became less challenging. One year later and coincidentally on New Year's Eve, I received news of my favorable win. God takes care of His children when they are unjustly targeted. Just like Joseph, God was with me. And He's with you as well. Justice may not come swiftly, but when God defends, you can guarantee that it will come.

## Prayer

*Dear Lord, thank you for being my great defender. You've seen the maltreatment I've experienced and I know you will fight for me. Please help me stand still and not run before you. In spite of my feelings, please help me forgive those whose intentions are to harm. I know that you will come through and give me justice at the right time. Give me the power to stand on your Truth. Amen.*

## DAY TEN REFLECTIONS

## DAY TEN REFLECTIONS

DAY 11

# Your Redeemer

*You were bought at a price. Therefore honor God with your bodies.*

1 Corinthians 6:20

Sold to the highest bidder. Christie's Auction house is one of the most world renowned and revered auction houses, selling only the finest art, homes, and jewelry one could imagined. Whether online or live at the auction, the room is always filled to capacity with each person wanting a piece of the action, an opportunity to be among the elite who owns one of the finest pieces one could acquire. Though I've never been to Christie's before, I can only imagine the daunting task of competing against others and paying top dollar for value. However, there is one who would love to see believers drown in a sea of self- pity as they struggle to believe their worth. Living in a society where competition is everything can leave even the most secure person feeling less than. Am I pretty enough? Too thin or too fat? Am I special or worthy of good things? Questions can linger, specifically for singles as they find themselves dateless yet again. As a result, self-talk may sound like reducing and comparing ones' value to others.

When you stand a chance of becoming the norm rather than the exception, the enemy's plan to separate you from God and believing what He's said about you has been achieved. But God. God's plan of redemption was won at Calvary. The love He has for you is so great that only an unblemished sacrifice would do. Therefore, He sent His Son to pay that price. Just for you.

To remove any barriers that would stand in the way of having an everlasting relationship with those He called His own. To think that you're less than because you're not married or "too anything," is offensive to God. Your value is wrapped in the blood and sacrifice of Jesus. Any good parent would want to lay down their life for their child. But you have an awesome parent: God, who paid the price with His son. Never doubt your worth, because God has redeemed you with an everlasting price.

## Prayer

*Dear Lord, Thank you for redeeming me. Thank you for sending your Son to save me. Forgive me for thinking I'm less than worthy or special because things in my life are not what I thought they would be. Help me to see myself the way you see me. Help me to let go of what I think I should be, and grab hold of what you desire me to be. I cannot do it without you. Lead me and guide me. Amen.*

## DAY ELVEN REFLECTIONS

## DAY ELEVEN REFLECTIONS

DAY 12

# Your Savior

*"Everyone who calls on the name of the Lord will be saved."*

Romans 10:13

It's all about who you know. If you want to get 'in,' you have to know the right people. How many times have we heard those words? People attend networking events and exchange numbers in hopes of capturing the attention of others and making their 'pitch.' A desire to be remembered through introduction, nice business cards, or eccentric personalities can lead you to building relationships that might not have occurred before. Knowing the right people can increase your status of that of your company. On the other hand, befriending individuals with a less than nice persona can negatively affect your standings with others. *He was known to be gentle, wise, and perfect.* Many miracles made Him popular with the crowd, while His teachings were questioned by the law. His skills and profession weren't something to brag about; His strength and power came from humility.

He was rejected, falsely accused, and mocked. Yet He still loved His enemies. He was the epitome of perfection and His name was Jesus. God's son, wrapped in flesh, and sent to save all. As children or adults, most are introduced to Him. However, something happens when the introduction becomes a rich experience leaving an unmistakable mark in your life. Most singles confess a deeper relationship with God happens after the demise of a relationship. Seeing Him as the lover of your soul seems easier, too, when hurt has been the anecdote.

When you come to the end of yourself, you find Him and discover He was there all along. Calling on Him to answer your deepest longings and cries, His saving grace gives you the strength to go on. On the quest to find love, you should realize that *true* love begins with God by accepting Jesus as your Savior. If the vertical relationship with Christ is not in sync, your horizontal relationship with others will be effected. God longs to be more than a networking experience. When you know and trust the One who makes your life matters, your status will always be on the upgrade.

## Prayer

*Dear Lord, thank you for saving me. Thank you for showing me the importance and purpose of knowing you. I submit to your leading and allow you to order my steps as you see fit. Please help me reflect who you are and draw those who don't know you. Your sacrifice on the cross and resurrection gives me life and meaning. Because I have you, I don't have to be concerned about popularity and status. Please help me see that in you, I have truth, love, and inspiration.*
*Amen.*

## DAY TWELVE REFLECTIONS

## DAY TWELVE REFLECTIONS

DAY 13

# Your Joy

> *"...And do not be grieved. For the joy of the Lord is your strength."*
>
> *Nehemiah 8:10*

There's a saying in the Church about joy—the world didn't give it and the world can't take it away! If joy was a scent, it would be a best seller. Many try to find and capture a moment or lifetime of this fragrance only to fall short. Emotions can fluctuate from happy to sad in a split second. A bad hand in life can quickly teach us about injustice and fairness. Truly, it's hard to find joy when our eyes see the ways of the world and the messy picture of our own lives. But we can draw from those mishaps and learn a great deal about God even in the midst of what we see. A great thing about having joy is that it's contagious. A look of glow, contentment, and peace can attract even the most unlikely critic and turn them into a fan. Circumstances can challenge us to question who we are and where our help comes from. Bad break ups, lousy bosses, boring jobs … we've all experienced that moment where "if only" seems to be the topic of the day.

However, no matter the situation, God is the only one who can give us a constant read when situations in our lives fluctuate. Having material things in our lives is not a prerequisite or requirement for joy. Most often, the *absence* of things can bring more fulfillment than ever. Joy can be found right here and right now. Why? Because He is the only One who can fill you and make you complete. And yes, it is an unspeakable joy! Embrace the joy right here and now in your season. It is the joy only He can give.

## Prayer

*Dear Lord, thank you for giving me joy. At times I forget that you are the one who makes life complete. Please help me to embrace the love and peace only you can truly bring. I want to wear your fragrance of joy. Please fill me up so that I want nothing less than you. Amen.*

## DAY THIRTEEN REFLECTIONS

## DAY THIRTEEN REFLECTIONS

DAY 14

# Your Light

*Your Word is a lamp to my feet and a light to my path.*

Psalm 119:105

It's difficult to find your way in the dark. Although your eyes may adjust to the room, there's nothing like having some light to guide the way. Your room may not appear physically dark, but a confused and wandering mind can bring about sleepless and restless nights. Lord, should I do this or go there? Should I date him/her? The questions can be relentless, causing us to question what God has already answered and doubt what we know to be true. I can recall a time in my journey of dating when praying about someone *before* the date even began gave me a sense of direction and prevented me from developing deeper feelings than I should have. Through a dream, God provided knowledge concerning that person and his intentions. God will illuminate and reveal the hearts and minds of others. Even more so, God will expose our agenda, which can be used to draw near to Him. So often, we're blinded by our own goodness and fail to see shortcomings. But God, as loving as He is, will hold the mirror and allow us to see the true reflection of our desires and intentions. If we want to be led into truth and discernment, allowing God to lead the way is always the way to go!

## Prayer

*Dear Lord, Thank you for being the light in the midst of darkness and confusion. Thank you for your unfailing love and grace that guides me into all truth and right paths for my life. You are all wonderful and wise, and never fail to lead me into greener pastures. I desire your will and guidance. Where you lead me, I will go. I would rather take one step with you than no step at all. Lord, I trust you are leading in my life and I thank you for doing so. Amen.*

## DAY FOURTEEN REFLECTIONS

## DAY FOURTEEN REFLECTIONS

DAY 15

# Your Hero

*God is our refuge and strength, an ever-present help in trouble.*

Psalm 46:1

A child sees a superhero figure in a cartoon and immediately becomes mesmerized by the hero's colors, cape, and ability to fly. Not knowing the word "hero," that child takes notice of the figure's ability to help and be kind to others. As we grow up, we take those same characteristics and apply them to those who've helped us along the way. Countless stories of gratitude, as tears convey the emotion experienced when sharing the words, "You saved my life," can make the greatest impact. No doubt about it, God has been my hero. What I once considered as frustrating and at times downright impossible, God has saved me from faulty thinking and wrong behaviors that could have set me on the wrong course. He saved me from myself and set me on a journey to freedom. It was in those moments where I fully understood and accepted my season of waiting (1 Corinthians 7:32). Through a small act of kindness or a big deed, we see the value and worth that person has, both in his or her life as well as in our own.

Without our "heros," our lives would be different and, for some, unbearable or nonexistent. Whether you find yourself healing from a break up or in condemnation from a mistake, God's balm can soothe your very heartache.

Through many experiences, God the Father, God the Son, and God the Holy Spirit—the magnificent Trinity—have also been our heroes. God the Father gave us His son Jesus to restore relationships with Him. After the death, resurrection, and ascension of Jesus, the Holy Spirit was left to comfort us daily.

They are One and it began with God the Father. He came to save the day by saving humanity. When you feel as though you can't go on and tears continue to fall, look to God who gave us One just to save us all.

## Prayer

*Dear Lord, Thank you for saving my life. In spite of my shortcomings, you still choose to forgive and rescue me. Thank you for your Son Jesus and the Holy Spirit who continues to be with me daily. Thank you for keeping me from seen and unseen danger. Thank you for picking me up when I fall and never letting me go. You are and forever will be my Hero. Amen.*

## DAY FIFTEEN REFLECTIONS

## DAY FIFTEEN REFLECTIONS

DAY 16

# Your Shield

> *In addition to all this, take up the shield of faith, with which you can extinguish all of the flaming arrows of the evil one. Take the helmet of salvation and the sword of the Spirit, which is the word of God.*
>
> Ephesians 6:16-17

Here's a stark reality. You will have to fight for your marriage. A marriage built on the foundation of God will always be target for the enemy. But what you may not have realized is that the fight doesn't begin when you get married. No. It began when you said yes to Jesus. Remember the game of dodge ball? As a child, you and your team would stand face-to-face with another team, each person trying to avoid being hit by the ball. The person with the ball had his or her eye on a specific target before throwing the ball, in hopes of hitting someone and being the last person standing. In this same way, the enemy has tried to distract, forfeit, and get you off target in your walk with Christ. The enemy works hard on destroying relationships through unforgiveness and projecting our pain on others. No wonder so many are walking around confused about their purpose and finding themselves stuck in relationships that were never ordained.

At any given cost, the enemy will try to get you to abort or give up what God has for you. If he can cause you to doubt God and take your eyes off Christ, then his agenda has served its purpose. But we have One who has fought for us, who is fighting for us, and who has already won!

How do you protect from getting trumped by the enemy? How do you protect and hold on to what's already promised to you? As the Bible says, we have to put on the full armor of God, so that we can stand against the devil's schemes (Ephesians 6:11, NIV). God is your shield. He protects you from danger and deception that the enemy throws your way.

God wants you suited up at all times to fight spiritually. He wants you ready and longs for you to use your weapons. One of your weapons is the shield of faith. The shield of faith is our protective barrier against schemes of the enemy and doubt.

This promise and guarantee is that we can believe God for His best in marriage, or the best case scenario if you're called to singleness. It places no exemption nor shows favoritism to ones' status. This shield is your lifeline, causing you to continue believing in the journey, in spite of what your eyes have not yet seen.

## Prayer

*Dear Lord, Thank you for being my shield of faith. Thank you for giving me the tools I need to fight for the life you've ordained for me and the support needed to do so. You have already fought and paid the price. Please help me to be mindful of the distractions the enemy will put in my way. I want to keep my eyes on you and believe you for the best outcome. Amen.*

## DAY SIXTEEN REFLECTIONS

## DAY SIXTEEN REFLECTIONS

DAY 17

# Your Love

*And may you have the power to understand, as all God's people should, how wide, how long, how high, and how deep his love is.*

Ephesians 3:18, NLT

While the dust settles on the dawn of a new year, many come to set their sights and marks on the next major holiday: Valentine's Day. For some, it can solidify and confirm the newness of romance or serve as a reminder of the importance of family and friends. For others, it highlights that another year has come without that special someone or promise manifested from God. Whether romantically or not, there's a longing we have to be chosen and remembered. To have someone take notice and desire quality time well spent. When major needs of love are not met, some may find themselves settling for crumbs instead of a full feast at the table. In the end, broken hearts and low expectations become difficult to resolve. In the attempt to include and appreciate singles on Valentine's Day, a new term called Single Awareness Day was introduced.

Though I'm not sure if it does more harm than good, this day highlights the basic human need of desire and love regardless of relational status. In the old testament, Jacob was tricked into marrying a young woman named Leah, whom he believed to be her younger sister, Rachel, the woman he truly loved.

The Bible makes it clear that beauty was not among the qualities that Leah possessed. Yet, she was the older sibling and it was customary for the eldest to marry first. Unbeknownst to Jacob, he didn't find out until his wedding night that he had in fact married Leah. Leah was not chosen. Jacob loved Rachel and he made no attempts to hide it. When the Lord saw that Leah was unloved, he enabled her to have children (Genesis 29:31, NLT). Rightly so, Leah desired the love from her husband. By having more children, Leah's attempt to capture that love failed (Genesis 29: 34).

After the birth of her last son, Leah's attempt to win Jacob's affection finally switched to God. She didn't have the love of her husband, but God didn't withhold his love for Leah. Her story is our story. Perhaps at one time or another we failed in an attempt to persuade or win the affection from those, whose love barometer didn't reach quite as high. But thanks be to God, He is not asking you to perform or persuade Him. There is no competition to win the love that He freely gives. He is already captivated by the very essence of you, because God created you, and you belong to Him.

## Prayer

*Dear Lord, Thank you for choosing and loving me. I don't have to persuade or compete for your attention. You love me because you created me. Thank you for not rejecting me, and for calling me your own. Please help me to continue finding my worth in you, no matter what. Amen.*

## DAY SEVENTEEN REFLECTIONS

## DAY SEVENTEEN REFLECTIONS

DAY 18

# Your Reward

*And without faith it is impossible to please God, because anyone who comes to him must believe that he exists and that he rewards those who earnestly seek him.*

*Hebrews 11:6*

Distracted. Busy. They're known to be the number one things that stand in the way of pursuing what really matters. So much so that distraction and business have become the enemy of knowing God intimately. Misplacing my cell phone has become more of a norm than I'd like to admit. On any given day, a frantic search for one of my most valued possessions is underway. Because my phone is used for multiple reasons, its value is ranked high. Having it near me takes precedent on my list of priorities. However, can we say the same in our relationship with God? Luke 10:38-42 tells about Jesus' visit to the home of two sisters, Mary and Martha. Excitement and anticipation got the best of Martha in preparing for His visit. So much so, that when He arrived Martha continued to focus on making sure every detail was in place. Perhaps she didn't think of preparation as neglectful, but it's obvious that He thought otherwise with His response: *But the Lord said to her, "My dear Martha, you are worried and upset over all these details! There is only one thing worth being concerned about. Mary has discovered it and it will not be taken away from her."* ( Luke 10: 41-42 NIV).

Despite the wonderful efforts to make her guest feel at home, Martha missed the essence of priorities. However, her sister Mary recognized the value of being present and engaging with her friend. As a result, a reward that included learning and deepening the best relationship that would never go out of style was being strengthened. Our moments in seeking God are often based on where our priorities lie. What I've found is that God is more concerned about consistent quality time than sporadic check-in's.

Even doing things *for* Him can stand in the way of being *with* Him. Recognizing that God's schedule is always free and available to us should ignite more intention and action to spend time with the One we love. God is waiting on us to carve out some time. Why? He longs to spend it with those He loves, telling them of things unknown. By giving Him our undivided attention and devotion, we can reap the rewards of guidance, peace, and answered prayers.

## Prayer

*Dear Lord, Thank you for choosing me. Thank you for wanting to spend time with me. Please forgive me for placing you last on my to do list. You deserve more than what I'm giving to you. I admit that lately, it's been easy to put other things and people before you. Please help me to desire and want you more than anything else. I need you to survive, and I will search and sit at your feet as I wait for your instructions.
Amen.*

## DAY EIGHTEEN REFLECTIONS

# DAY EIGHTEEN REFLECTIONS

DAY 19

# Your Heart Keeper

*And the peace of God, which transcends all understanding, will guard your hearts and your minds in Christ Jesus.*

Philippians 4:7

You made a mistake ... again. Leaving your heart open to the wrong person and perhaps at the wrong time. *This* time would be different, or so you thought. As you sit rehashing the time and emotional investment it cost you, God is there, waiting for you to give Him your most precious gift—your heart. The feelings of euphoria and possibilities of love open the door for us to give without wisdom. I'm reminded of Hollywood's most iconic night: the Oscars. Each year, stars grace the red carpet with beautiful gowns and jewels. While we see many starlets being asked the famous question—who are you wearing—many do not see the bodyguards whose sole purpose is to guard the jewels. These expensive jewels are kept close to the representative at all times. Ensuring safety, beauty, and integrity, the responsibility of the guards is to make sure jewels are returned in the same condition the owner has given it. So it is with our hearts. God considers His children heirs and royalty.

Because we were bought with a price, our value in Christ is worth more than gold. God knows who we should embrace and who we should avoid. He knows that we can be easily led astray, only to return back to Him bruised and battered from placing our hearts in the wrong hands. Because of this, God desires his children to place their hearts in His hand.

He desires to protect us from the elements of confusion, lust, and maltreatment from others. In addition, God protects us from ourselves. Knowing how to discern, utilizing wisdom, as well as our feelings can lead us in the right direction. Feelings alone can be deceitful (Jeremiah 17:9). What appears to be loving and true may be a façade. Allowing God to protect our hearts will give us the peace and rest our fragile hearts have been longing for. Won't you let Him protect you as your ultimate guard?

## Prayer

*Dear Lord, Thank you for protecting my heart. Forgive me for not being led by you, trusting that you know what's best for my life. Please heal me from relationships and situations I've naively placed myself in. I now want to place my heart in your Hands for safe keeping. I trust that you will lead, protect, and place me in the right hands ... when the time is right. Thank you, Lord. Amen.*

## DAY NINETEEN REFLECTIONS

## DAY NINETEEN REFLECTIONS

DAY 20

# Your Potter

*But the pot he was shaping was marred in his hands; so the potter formed it into another pot, shaping it as it seemed best to him. Then the word of the Lord came to me. He said, "Can I not do with you, Israel, as this potter does?" declares the Lord. "Like clay in the hand of the potter, so are you in my hand, Israel."*

Jeremiah 18:4-6

Home makeover shows are all the rage. There's just something about seeing homes transformed into their fullest potential. From before to after, we get more than a glimpse of what could be. Rather, we're moved to go beyond the old way of things and say hello to new beginnings. With the right designer, a keen eye is trained to fix the broken and create the new. While we all can relate to having a broken heart, I often wonder if Joseph's heart was shattered from the treatment of his brothers. After all, if they had not sold him into slavery his story might not have included time in prison. The betrayal of family members can hurt, and entrusting those you love with your heart can often backfire, leaving you with feelings of rejection, vulnerability, and hopelessness as you try to pick up the pieces. That's what happened to me. A key love relationship gone wrong taught me just how fragile the heart is.

Depression became a long lost friend as days and years went by. Likewise, songs and memories left a sting that reminded me of moments long gone. While it appeared as if things were okay, "My house" was in shambles on the inside. I was desperate and in need of *something*. As my pillow became a shoulder to cry on during many nights, hearing the words "I love you" from God began my journey of healing.

What I failed to realize at that moment was that God, the perfect designer, had been waiting to put the pieces back together. That's what He longs to do for you. A touch from God is always transformative, creating newness out of the old and dead things.

Extreme makeovers is not a new concept to God. In fact, I believe He delights in them. With God, all things can be made new! While the job of a potter includes examining every inch of his vessel, God is concerned about the condition of your heart. When you're broken, God is the perfect mender to take what you have and create a beautiful masterpiece. Surely broken things can be made beautiful when you place your heart in His hands. As I finally gave

Him the fragments of my heart, God gave me hope and belief that all was not lost and a better future awaits. Place your heart in His hands and allow Him to transform your tears into an awesome testimony for His glory.

## Prayer

*Dear Lord, Thank you for being the Potter. I admit that my brokenness has gotten the best of me. At times, the heaviness of my heart speaks louder than your promise to love and take care of me. Please help me to give you every shattered piece, entrusting that you can do something better than I ever could. In moments like these it is difficult to trust anyone. But you're just not anyone, you are Lord. Please walk with me on this journey of healing. God, I give you my heart. I give you all of me. Amen.*

## DAY TWENTY REFLECTIONS

## DAY TWO REFLECTIONS

DAY 21

# Your Healer

*...And provide for those who grieve in Zion- to bestow on them a crown of beauty instead of ashes, the oil of joy instead of mourning, and a garment of praise, instead of a spirit of despair. They will be called oaks of righteousness, a planting of the Lord for the display of his splendor.*

Isaiah 61:3

A broken heart and sickness share the same remedy: Jesus. So many times we hear about healing as it relates to physical infirmities. You may believe that God only heals those who've been given a diagnosis or bad report from the doctor. But He is God and His healing includes both physical and emotional scars. Your wounds may be evident to some, while deeper wounds lie within. I recall a time when healing from a break up took longer than I'd like to admit. I was looking to quickly get over someone, yet God wanted to transform my life by starting at the root of my hurt. God walked with me through each pain, wrong ideology, and sadness that hindered my future. His method of deep cleaning cannot be assumed or identical to the stories of others. For some, the journey of healing takes time.

Who better to heal and walk with you than the author of time? God desires to take all that concerns you and breathe new life into every hurt and scar you possess. Whether your scars are self-inflicted or from the negligence of others, God's ultimate will is for your healing to take place as you move forward and live for Him. God can turn your mistake into a masterpiece and pain into a beautiful testimony, giving honor to His name and helping those in need. You'll never be put to shame when you're vulnerable with God and release your hurts. No matter what report you've been given, believe the report of the Lord. God is a healer.

## Prayer

*Dear Lord, I come to you with so much pain in my life and need your healing. Your Word says by your stripes I am healed. Although I may not physically see it yet, I have faith in you and what you will accomplish in my life. You are the only One who can heal me like no other. Father, I bring you my pain in exchange for your grace. I trust you in choosing the way for healing in my life. Whether instantly or day by day, I know that one word from you is all I need. Thank you for your love, patience, and healing. Amen.*

## DAY TWENTY-ONE REFLECTIONS

## DAY TWENTY-ONE REFLECTIONS

DAY 22

# Your Strength

*And he said to me, "My grace is sufficient for you, for my strength is made perfect in weakness."*

2 Corinthians 12:9

L ife is hard. Though we may not want to admit it, there are moments when *we* make life harder than it has to be. I heard someone say once, "if you've never been through anything, just keep on living." No matter our upbringing or beliefs, we can all attest to the challenge of keeping our head above water. You may be bombarded by relationships gone wrong (or the lack thereof), difficulties on the job or at school, or just plain ole life transitions. It would be so easy to buckle under pressure. To allow the weight of life and distractions to have the final say. But God. His load is never full and He's not complained yet. I've heard many people remark about how easy life can be when you're single- with or without children. Although I'm not married and without children, I can certainly attest to a *different* kind of pressure many in my shoes face. At one time, the weight of school, work, and taking care of loved ones had taken its toll.

I experienced burnout and worry from a plethora of concerns. Because of that stress, I entertained thoughts of quitting school. Finally, with very little strength, I cried out to God for help and spoke to Him as I would a friend. In return, God's supernatural strength empowered me to continue doing the assignment and role for that season.

The God who created the world and everything in it is more than capable of taking your problem and adding it to *His* to-do list. Why? Because He loves us so! Instead of seeing your problems as insurmountable, grab onto His promise. God knows just how much you're able to bear, more than you think. He is strong and mighty. Is there anything too hard for God? No. Delight in His strength, and cling to His promise. Your burdens will feel lighter as you focus on His strength instead of your problems.

## Prayer

*Dear Lord, Thank you for being a burden bearer. Forgive me for losing sight of you in the midst of my challenges. You have taken care of me before and lightened my load. I know that my problems are small compared to what you're able to do with them. Lord, I give you my weaknesses and burdens. I'm trusting you to carry me and give me the strength I need to go on. Thank you for reminding me of your strength and ability to carry the weight of the world. Amen.*

## DAY TWENTY-TWO REFLECTIONS

## DAY TWENTY-TWO REFLECTIONS

DAY 23

# Your Restorer

> *I will restore to you the years that the swarming locust has eaten, the hopper, the destroyer, and the cutter, my great army, which I sent among you.*
>
> Joel 2:25, ESV

There's nothing more satisfying than hearing about testimonies of families and friendships restored. The reconciliation seems to bring an awareness that people can change for the better when healing takes place. It's no secret that the goal of the enemy includes division, among other things. If he can tear or dismantle a Godly relationship or opportunity to witness, half the battle is over. Besides our own human fallacies, I believe the enemy works overtime to cause strife in relationships. The character of God, witnessing, and discipleship is utilized in our relationships with others. When we unite, we are strengthened and encouraged to continue our walk with Christ and love each other. However, when we are at odds, all parties involved are vulnerable and open to more attacks spiritually. Words said to a friend almost threatened to end the story of friendship in our lives. To this day, I cannot recall the exact words that ignited from false assumptions. However, I can remember the feelings and look from my friend after the mistake was made.

Unbeknownst to me, it took some time to realize the impact of what was said. On the outside, it appeared as if the friendship was over but God had other plans. Confirmation of restoration of our relationship was given to me through dreams and a spoken word from someone I'd just met. I knew God was saying the relationship would be restored.

However, it certainly happened in His time and His way. During our season apart, feelings of hurt and unforgiveness had to be dealt with for the both of us. Almost a year later, new beginnings started to spring forth as we took steps to build our friendship again. Even in our errors, God can use anything and work it out for the ultimate good (Romans 8:28).

God restores broken marriages and friendships because they are extensions of His love for us. You were never meant to live this life alone, in isolation trying to figure things out for yourself. When God restores, He builds relationships better than before. You may never forget the details or exact cause of the break. However, you'll be able to testify about the power of His promise and defeat of the enemy.

## Prayer

*Dear Lord, thank you for your restorative power. Thank you for placing my family and friends in my life. I realize their love and care is only a small fraction of how you feel about me. But I thank you for mending our broken relationship and building it back up, the way you desire it to be. Please help and give me the tools to maintain the gifts of family and friends. I want to be a great blessing to those you place in my life. Amen.*

## DAY TWENTY-THREE REFLECTIONS

# DAY TWENTY-THREE REFLECTIONS

DAY 24

# Your Answer

*If any of you lacks wisdom, you should ask God, who gives generously to all without finding fault, and it will be given to you,*

James 1:5

If you've got a problem in your life, take it to Jesus. Though I remember hearing that song as a child, I hadn't yet fathomed the power and truth of those words until I became an adult. Throughout time, people have searched for purpose and the meaning of life. The industry of mediums and psychics are not new to modern day. Even in biblical times kings and others searched the stars and minds of magicians, looking for answers to their most haunting questions. Just like today, being so quick and eager to know what the future holds, many flock to others with the belief that they hold the keys to their answer. The Bible has many scriptures, encouraging us to wait on God for the answer. Yet in our microwave society, the ability to wait has become a lost art. The consequences of not waiting on God's answer can result in missed opportunities and disobedience. Lord, should I date this person or seek this job opportunity? We ask Him, but are we ready for the answer He'll give to us?

If you ask, God will show you how to be stewards in your call to singlehood, just as God gives instructions on marriage. There will be a grace to handle whatever gift He has called you to. I prayed about a relationship once and with confidence said, "Lord if this is not your will, remove this guy from my life." The very next day I received a phone call from that young man, stating he thought it best that we should remain friends. Talk about fast! I wanted an answer, but surely wasn't prepared for that one and so soon. Truth be told, I really didn't want to let go. But God answered.

In His sovereignty, He knew what lie ahead if I went down that road. When you come boldly to Him in prayer and reverential respect, you can ask and receive His answer in His timing. Whether the answer is no, wait, or yes, we can trust that our Father has our best interest at heart.

## Prayer

*Dear Lord, thank you for always having the answers. I may not understand them all or the need to wait, but I trust that you know best. Thank you for always having my best interest in mind. I realize you want the best for my life, more than I'm able to comprehend. Help me to always seek you for the answer and trust your timing to provide it. Amen.*

## DAY TWENTY-FOUR REFLECTIONS

# DAY TWENTY-FOUR REFLECTIONS

DAY 25

# Your Advocate

*.... But if anyone does sin, we have an advocate who pleads our case before the Father.*

1 John 2:1, NLT

A guilty verdict. Let's face it, we all deserve to have one. Even in our best attempts to be right or perfect, we still fall short. We can strive for perfection, but knowing that we'll never reach the top of that mountain should give a healthy dose of reality. Plain and simple, there's just no such thing as a perfect Christian. Going down memory lane to high school, I clearly recall a time when my grades were *less* than perfect. However, the great opportunity to be mentored in a program for future doctors gave me such excitement that I applied despite of not meeting GPA requirements. I would like to believe that great essay writing skills alone is what afforded me to be accepted. However, I was sadly mistaken. I'll never forget the words said to me, "We pleaded on your behalf for your acceptance, because your grades did not qualify you to attend. You have the potential and your essay is evidence. But, it wasn't easy." In that phone call, I knew that someone pleaded my case and saw something more.

On that day, I was grateful. Her words with the director concerning my aptitude sealed the deal and solidified my presence with others who strived for more as well. So many find themselves coloring outside the lines of God's boundaries.

We know what we should do. However, the persuasion to sin looks more appealing and attractive than being confined to limitations. Because God knows our human instinct and proclivity to sin, He provided an answer: God's son, Jesus, as our mediator.

He is our advocate and goes before God to plead our case. Securing a verdict of not guilty for us is His goal. His role of advocating for us is continuous, because of our need to repent and confess daily.

*Not* meeting the standard of perfection should put your mind at ease, because we have One who goes before us, advocating to restore a right relationship with God and seal your reservation to spend eternity with Him.

## Prayer

*Dear Lord, thank you for being my advocate. I know that I am less than perfect and will never reach perfection. Thank you for not asking me to do so. Thank you for understanding my desire to serve you isn't always shown in what I do. I ask for your forgiveness and accept it by faith. Please help and give me the desire to honor you with my speech and behavior. Thank you for giving me another chance to get it right and not giving me what I deserve. Amen.*

## DAY TWENTY-FIVE REFLECTIONS

# DAY TWENTY-FIVE REFLECTIONS

DAY 26

# Your Creator

*For you created my inmost being; you knit me together in my mother's womb. I praise you because I am fearfully and wonderfully made; your works are wonderful, I know that full well. My frame was not hidden from you when I was made in the secret place, when I was woven together in the depths of the earth. Your eyes saw my unformed body; all the days ordained for me were written in your book before one of them came to be.*

Psalm 139:13-16

Not only did God create the world, but He formed you. Specifically, and uniquely. No one could ever speak, think, or feel the way you do. Our DNA is the one thing that sets everyone apart. No one will laugh or smile exactly like you because you were made to be different. Not only does your DNA set you apart, being a child of God sets you apart even more so. As days and years of being single stare you in the face, questions of distinctiveness often set in. Perhaps you're believing lies that question your appearance, intelligence, or personality: "If I had "this," maybe I would have "that." While there's always room to grow and become better in every aspect, allowing the enemy to plant seeds of doubt and question God's masterpiece will stunt your growth.

If you didn't know by now, YOU are God's masterpiece and mistakes are not a part of His character. The gifts and talents He put on the inside of you are uniquely yours. No one can do what you can! God knows you better than you know yourself. You are God's biggest investment, because your soul is at stake.

He delights in His creation, realizing that we're all in need of saving and yet loving us still. Rest in the knowledge that He who created the world can take your life and create something new. He has not been outdone and will never be. God has the power to transform all that He's created before and make it new again. Let all the created worship the Creator.

## Prayer

*Dear Lord, Thank you for creating me so delicately and with such great love. Though I am not what I should be, you created a wonderful masterpiece for your glory. Please help me to remain in humble submission to You. You know the thoughts and words I speak before I even speak them. Yet still, You continue to show patience and love toward your creation. I pray that I never lose sight of my ultimate purpose, to worship You, my Creator and Lord. Thank you Father, your works are marvelous. Amen.*

## DAY TWENTY-SIX REFLECTIONS

## DAY TWENTY-SIX REFLECTIONS

DAY 27

# Your Portion

*My flesh and heart may fail, but God is the strength of my heart and my portion forever.*

Psalm 73:26

"Give us this day our daily bread." God knows what we need, when we're in need, and just how much to give. He's a God of overflowing blessings and more than enough. Yet, in our blessings He gives us what we're capable of handling. Stop and take a good look at your life. The blessings and prayers that you're asking for—is there enough room to fit them in? I recall being fortunate enough to be in graduate school, and without a husband or child to compete for my attention. My life was certainly full. I found myself thanking God for what I *didn't* have, which was a stark contrast to complaining about what I lacked before. Your cup may look different than mine. Perhaps filled to the brim or somewhere in the middle. Regardless, we ask Him for *more*. More time, money, and relationships, whatever our heart's desire.

Believing that we're ready to handle what we're praying for. Yet, in this season God is showing us that He's more than enough. For He loves us too much to give us anything more than what is needed at the moment. His love is far too great to give us more than what our feelings crave.

So, He gives us exactly what we need: More of Him, which, in fact, we can never have enough of. He desires to fill our cups with more of Him, so that we lack nothing in our next place of promise.

## Prayer

*Dear Lord, thank you for being my portion. Thank you for being all that I need. You know the desires of my heart and have promised to fulfill them. Please help me to be content with the portion you've given me. I may not fully understand, but in your wisdom, you know what I need at this moment and what I can handle. You are my portion and my life. Lord, I trust in you. Amen.*

## DAY TWENTY-SEVEN REFLECTIONS

## DAY TWENTY-SEVEN REFLECTIONS

DAY 28

# Your Comfort

An unnecessarily long relationship finally came to an end. "He'll never break my heart," were the words said so many years ago. To my surprise, the perfect match on paper was anything but. Christian, kind, intelligent, you name it. The important attributes were present. But mothers can spot a charmer when they see it. While I was blinded by characteristics, one vital thing was not included in my assessment. He just wasn't *that* into me. All the right words were said, but actions didn't match up. At the end, my fragmented heart proved difficult to rebuild as God walked me through years of healing. Day by day, God met me at what I considered my lowest and comforted me with His silence. To be honest, I wasn't sure If I was ready to hear from God. Knowing where I wanted to be and realizing His answer of 'no' proved to be too difficult to comprehend at the moment. Therefore, His silence of comfort was all that my heart could handle. After anger subsided and feelings of hurt lingered, His love and nearness brought me even closer to accepting that my choice was not God's best. I became aware that I was truly meeting God for the first time. Through this pain of rejection, I was finally open to God's leading and comfort in my life. God doesn't promise us days of carefree living.

The great thing about discomfort is the promise that God will make good use of it. Our mishaps, mistakes, and pain can be used to get us to the place He's calling us to. Even in our pain, God's promise of never leaving us still remains. Ever.

Allow God to wrap His arms around the pain, confusion, and silence of wonder. God hears the longings and cries of hearts and yours is not exempt. Not today, not ever.

## Prayer

*Dear Lord, Thank you for comforting me. In times of distress, you have proven over and over that your understanding and healing balm is enough. In your silence, I trust that your ears have heard my request. You never sleep and you never fail to hear me when I call. Through my discomfort, you have shown that you are near and that you care about what concerns me. Thank you for your everlasting love and comforting touch. Amen.*

## DAY TWENTY-EIGHT REFLECTIONS

## DAY TWENTY-EIGHT REFLECTIONS

DAY 29

# Your Peace

*And the peace of God which transcends all understanding, will guard your hearts and minds in Christ Jesus.*

Philippians 4:7

Control freak and Type A personality. Headaches used to plague me because of senseless worrying. Being afraid to fully surrender my life to God consumed a large portion of my time as a young adult. I relied on my lists—my visual of goals and desires that were always within reach—in place of God. Prior to fully trusting God with my life, fear of the unknown consumed me and was the reason I held onto my plan so tightly. But God was asking me to walk in faith, trusting Him with *the* plan for my life. Thoughts of giving up my desire for the unseen and gain something greater from God, was a step of faith that I did not readily embrace. Yet, the temptation to forgo peace while waiting on His promise seemed to conflict as well.

Sarah and Abraham waited years for their promised son, Isaac. One of their biggest challenges was choosing to remain in peace during the midst of waiting. Evidence for their lack of trust and peace in God's promise was found in recruiting Hagar to bear a son for Abraham and Sarah. The promise from God was theirs.

It was settled with Him and repeated to them more than once. God's promise for a son was guaranteed. However, time has a way of refining and showing our character as we wait. They had no control over what God promised. Yet, they had control in choosing the peace of God.

Trusting in God gives you peace. Having peace means you are trusting in the sovereignty of God. A relationship with God is reflected in our trust. Many times in His Word, He reminds us of His ability to answer prayers, keep His promises, and take care of His children.

This invitation to peace is also a recommendation to trust. In Him, you can find peace no matter the storm or length of the wait. Letting God be Lord over your life does not excuse anyone from the harsh realities that may await. Yet, the peace of God can cause you to sing in the rain as you wait.

## Prayer

*Dear Lord, Thank you for the peace that surpasses all understanding. I may not know what's going to happen next and admit this causes me fear. Thank you for loving me in spite of my fears with an invitation to take hold of your peace. I believe your plan is great for my life in spite of what I can see. I ask that you take away this fear and give me your peace and trust in you. Help me Lord, to make the choice to let go of worry and choose your peace instead. Amen.*

## DAY TWENTY-NINE REFLECTIONS

## DAY TWENTY-NINE REFLECTIONS

DAY 30

# Your Shepherd

> *The sheep hear his voice, and he calls his own sheep by name and leads them out. When he has brought out all his own, he goes before them, and the sheep follow him, for they know his voice.*
>
> John 10:4

I knew God had said no to *this* relationship. He gave me every indication that something wasn't right. I knew His voice and yet I chose to go in the opposite direction. Many can recall moments of regret when making a mental re-cap on relationships gone wrong. Uncomfortable feelings or words give us clear indication that we're headed in the wrong direction. After some time had passed, meeting someone whom I instantly knew was a "bad idea" turned into a year of being outside the will of God. Repeatedly, God had shown and warned me of the person *I'd* chosen, being nowhere near His best and will. Yet, I chose to remain. At last, seeing a glimpse of myself apologizing to God in a dream for *not* listening, was the beginning of the end. Analogies of shepherd and sheep are used in the Bible to give examples of how believers are dependent upon the shepherd as their guide.

It's no surprise that sheep are known to have excellent hearing and a great sense of following directions. Because of their vulnerability, they solely rely on the shepherd's guidance, provision, and protection. Without a good leader, they would be lost. Sounds a lot like us! A good shepherd always leads his sheep to greener pastures or better opportunities.

We want to be led, but can we recognize a good shepherd when we see one? Reflect on how God has covered and led you thus far. He's already displayed His characteristics that would make following and obeying Him without fear more than possible.

His wisdom, dependability, and care gives you all the more reason to trust Him with each step along the way. By following God, who is your shepherd, you can be content in knowing He will never lead you astray and will walk beside you (Psalm 23).

## Prayer

*Dear Lord, thank you for being my shepherd. You have guided me and led me on the best paths. Forgive me for going astray and rebelling. When I try to lead my own life, I always come up short. I will always be led in the wrong direction when I go without you. Please help me to continue on the path you have set for me. I know you have my best interest at heart. I need you to survive. Amen.*

## DAY THIRTY REFLECTIONS

## DAY THIRTY REFLECTIONS

DAY 31

# Your Load Bearer

*Cast all your anxiety on him, because he cares for you.*

1 Peter 5:7

Self-care has become a top priority for me. Massages have become a needed monthly ritual due to my stressful work in the public sector. Just the thought of scheduling my time has become the prescription to my need of taking the load off. Like clockwork, the masseuse would say that tension found in my neck, shoulders, and back, were tighter than it should be. The challenge to relax while being overworked became the obstacle I tried to overcome. I've found that loads come in all shapes and sizes. Some could be seen, but most of the time can go unnoticed by many—except the person who's doing the carrying. Loads of unforgiveness, anger, bitterness, mounting responsibilities ... the list can go on and on. If left unchecked, these loads affect our spiritual walk, our speech, relationships with others, and interaction with Christ. There's no way around it: carrying unnecessary loads will weigh you down.

While driving from Church one day, I poured out to Him the weight that threatened to take me under. Unforgiveness—with a church member. I can still recall the hurt and shock, it all being so great. As time passed, I found myself still under the weight of unforgiveness, while bitterness was right around the corner. God responded very clearly: "Give it to me."

So simple and yet so profound. That's what I decided to do in that moment. Instantly, I was set free! God wants that freedom for you as well. There is One who is more than ready to lift your load. God doesn't want you to be bombarded by trials or unforgiveness.

He wants your mind and heart clear to remain in forgiveness and fellowship with Him. Carrying a load bears the great consequence of coming between you, your growth, and Christ. He doesn't want that. Give it to Him. He's not intimidated by it and can carry your load no matter the size.

## Prayer

*Dear Lord, Thank you for wanting to carry my loads. I admit it's been too much to bear. Thank you for soothing me in my hurts. I know that you don't want me to stay there. Help me to release the person or situation that has caused me to lose sight of your grace. You've forgiven me and I want to forgive others just the same. I need you to help me rise above the hurt and extend mercy as you've extended to me. Amen.*

## DAY THIRTY-ONE REFLECTIONS

# DAY THIRTY-ONE REFLECTIONS

DAY 32

# Your Rest

*He who dwells in the shelter of the Most High will abide in the shadow of the almighty*

Psalms 91:1

Fear. Anxiousness. Worry. They are known to be enemies of resting in God. If you've ever seen the look of rest on babies and small children as they sleep, you may have become a bit envious of their ability to sleep deeply among all that's happening around them. With no cares in the world, they shake off all that happened during the day as they get ready to embrace the new beginnings of tomorrow. There was a time where concern about when God would bring my soulmate on the scene grew out of hand. *When, God, when?* What's taking so long? On the inside, silent adult tantrums became a norm. However, one night God answered me during a dream with two words: Just Rest. *Just*

*Rest*. The next morning, I continued to recall the dream that provided me with some relief. Through that dream, God was showing me that He cared and He had an answer that could help me shake off the fear and wasteful time of misery.

I no longer had doubt that God was going to fulfill the promise. Choosing to rest in God's timing provided me the relief I was looking for. I didn't have to peer around God's shoulder trying to see when the promises would come.

Rather, I nestled into God's rest with assurance that yes, it's coming. That's when I began to look forward to marriage, being whole and secure in Christ.

Many singles also find themselves in the same predicament of constant worry. Specifically, when it comes to who God will send and when. Whatever your situation is, never ending stress about details that are already taken care of is telling of our refusal to enter His rest.

Resting in God is not equated with acting passively. However, choosing to enter His rest is telling of our trust in Him to handle what we deem to be so dear. In the Bible, Jesus questions the disciples when they feared the raging storm on the sea (Matthew 8:24-26). As Jesus slept on deck, they woke Him up and cried out, saying, "Lord save us, we're going to drown." Jesus' response was simply, "why are you so afraid?"

Just like the disciples, we already have Jesus on board with us. He's orchestrating our lives for the best and His ultimate good. God is still asking that question today: "Why are you so afraid?" Just rest. He has it all under control.

## Prayer

*Dear Lord, Thank you for having my life in your Hands. Thank you for having everything under control, no matter how things may look in my life. Lord, I want to enter your rest, but sometimes find it hard to do so. Forgive me for stressing about things more than trusting you in them. I want to trust you with my whole heart. Help me choose your sweet rest, not just in this season, but in each day of my life.
Amen.*

# DAY THIRTY-TWO REFLECTIONS

## DAY THIRTY-TWO REFLECTIONS

DAY 33

# Your Provider

*And my God shall supply all of your needs, according to His riches and glory by Christ Jesus.*

Philippians 4:19, NKJV

Life happens. Sickness, loss of job, and mounting bills can all find their way to your doorstep without advance notice, causing many sleepless nights and worry as you question how it can all be worked out. When you don't have the means to accommodate yourself and those in your care, panic usually sets in, sounding off the internal alarm of frustration and fear. Taking the leap from full-time employment to full-time doctoral student was a leap I took that was guided by God. In the beginning of the year, I had no previous knowledge that stepping out in faith in this instant would be a season of coming to know Him as provider like never before. Ten years had already gone by with a constant stream of income that provided much comfort. The safety net that I had grown accustomed to was no longer. Now, I was being stretched and called to view God from a new perspective. Not only did I need HIM to help me navigate this new time of being a student, but daily responsibilities had to be maintained.

What I didn't realize was that my act of obedience in applying for school funding months before, would be the very thing He used to assist me in this new undertaking while unemployed. God was ordering my steps to meet this financial need, before I even knew there would be a need months later! There's a saying that rings true, "God has been where you're going and He's gone where you've been." He can take something so little and meet the needs of many within seconds. God is not surprised at your current circumstances. His provisions don't begin the moment you're in need.

God already knows our needs before they even appear to be a need. He is a provider who is concerned about His children and has promised to take care of them. Trust that God will provide whatever your need is. No matter how small or how large, our Father owns the world and His supply will never run out.

## Prayer

*Dear Lord, Thank you for meeting my needs. You have taken such good care of me and provided in times of lack. I know you care and trust that I will not lack what I need to take care of myself and family. Lord, I trust that you will meet my needs in your timing. Thank you for stretching my faith and seeing you as the Father who always provides for His children. Amen.*

## DAY THIRTY-THREE REFLECTIONS

## DAY THIRTY-THREE REFLECTIONS

DAY 34

# Your Grace

*For by grace you have been saved through faith, and not that of yourselves; it is the gift of God, not of works, lest anyone should boast. For we are His workmanship, created in Christ Jesus for Good works, which God prepared beforehand that we should walk in them.*

Ephesians 2:8-10

Grace: The free and unmerited favor of God. We can't earn it, manipulate, or perform extra tasks to receive it. We just don't deserve it. Without it, our lives would be full of doom and chaos. But with it, we have yet another chance to start over and make it right. How many times have we fallen short of what we *should* be doing according to God's standards? Known as the adulterous woman in the Bible, this woman had been caught in the act of adultery. According to the law at that time, stoning her to death would be the aftermath of her affair. As the Pharisees asked God about what should be done (in hopes of tricking Him), God used that teachable moment to remind them no one is exempt from falling. "All right but let the one who has never sinned throw the first stone!" (John 8:7). In one moment, His grace was displayed as He suggested at one time or another, they too were given extensions of mercy. That woman didn't deserve vindication, but God gave it to her. Where would she be if He didn't grant her grace? Where would *we* be?

Vows or promises made to God in hopes of ending habitual sin or continuing in empty relationships are often not kept. While the intentions may be noble, the execution or plan to change appear harder than we'd thought. But God steps in with His mercy to give us all another chance.

To forgive us in our failures when true repentance escapes from our lips and onto His heart. The same grace displayed back then continues to be given today. God has already gotten a sneak peak of our failures and needs before one of them comes to be.

In the midst of our triumphs and trials, it's a blessing to know that compassion instead of condemnation is given from God. He doesn't condone our sins or mishaps, but He is willing and ready to forgive us in our wrongdoings.

## Prayer

*Dear God, Thank you for your grace. I'm not deserving of all that you've given to me, but I thank you for seeing me beyond my failures. Thank you for your compassion and forgiveness. Please help me to continue being obedient and living according to your will and standards. I don't want to take your grace for granted. I ask that you continue to keep me as I remain in your presence. Amen.*

## DAY THIRTY-FOUR REFLECTIONS

## DAY THIRTY-FOUR REFLECTIONS

DAY 35

# Your Hope

*Against all hope, Abraham in hope believed and so became the father of many nations, just as it had been said to him, "So shall your offspring be."*

Romans 4:18

If God didn't exist, there would be no reason to hope. Hope defined is a feeling of expectation. A feeling of trust. When you look around the world and around your city, I'm sure you can find many reasons to give up. Even in your own day to day, with uncertainty and disappointments, you can find a justified reason to throw in the towel. "You've given up on God." Those words said by my father, as I wore a look of hopelessness on my face. Startled by his assessment, I knew it to be true. I'd never discussed with him what was going on. Yet, feeling as though God was speaking to me with those words, a small seed of hope was planted by my father's words that day. Many single women find themselves concerned with the lack of available suitors. But as you think about all He's done for you and the lives of others, you cling to hope. Hope isn't just a four letter word that can easily be thrown aside.

Hope is packed with possibility, promise, and assurance that even in the midst of a fallen world, all will be well. Because God *is* Hope. Hope gives us a reason to wake up and keep going in spite of the unseen winds. Hope allows us to be stretched more than we believed we could handle. Hope gives us the energy and fortitude to keep on fighting.

That's what God does and that's who He is. He is our blessed Hope. The One who calls us to trust in Him daily. No. Matter. What. Keep Hope alive and stay connected to God, who is our blessed hope.

## Prayer

*Dear Lord, Thank you for being my everlasting hope. You are the reason that I live and continue to show up when I want to give up. Thank you for reminding me that time is In your Hands. No matter what season you've allowed me to experience, please help me to keep hope alive. Trusting in you to deliver your promises when the time is right. Amen.*

## DAY THIRTY-FIVE REFLECTIONS

## DAY THIRTY-FIVE REFLECTIONS

DAY 36

# Your Source

> *"Here is a boy with five small barley loaves and two small fish, but how far will they go among so many?" .... Jesus then took the loaves, gave thanks, and distributed to those who were seated as much as they wanted. He did the same with the fish.*
>
> John 6:9, 11

Five loaves of bread and two fish. Many would consider it impossible to feed five thousand men alone, not counting the addition of women and children. The disciples had a dilemma. Being told by Jesus to feed the crowd, they looked at what they had and asked Him how it could be done. Can you blame them? We can all relate to seasons of lack. One's faith can be shaken when the list of needs are larger than your bank account. But there is more to consider. God already knew how many were present that day, how much the disciples could afford, and how much food was readily available (John 6:5-9). And yet, the instructions given appear to contradict what they could do with what they had. Throughout the Bible, God is often seen giving instructions that seem impossible. From downsizing an army to fight (and win), to asking Abraham to sacrifice his promised son, His ways appear to contradict who He is.

But God has a plan and He is always purposeful in doing so. If you didn't know by now, living a life in God is full of adventure. If you like spontaneity, hang on and enjoy the ride. However, if you're anything like me the unknown can be downright scary. But isn't that what faith is all about? The disciples had God at their disposal and He was the only One who could make much from little. As you take a survey of your life, what is God asking or rather telling you to do? This season can be full of unknowns, ranging from job transitions to lack of funds to new relationships. The list can go on. Just like the disciples, God is calling you to trust Him to do what He does best: Make it happen.

God can surely take what you have and multiply it. When you give God your little through obedience, your return on investment is bigger than what you started with. He is the only One who will never run out of resources, because He is The Source.

## Prayer

*Thank you, Lord, for being the Source. You have taken care of me when I could not see how. Forgive me for my lack of faith. You make the impossible happen in spite of how much I have to give. You are the one who can make more than enough. Please help me to see your Hand more than I see my circumstances. Your resources are limitless. Thank you for using this uncomfortable time to see another side of You. I know that you'll continue to take care of me, as you've done before. Amen.*

## DAY THIRTY-SIX REFLECTIONS

## DAY THIRTY-SIX REFLECTIONS

DAY 37

# Your Deliverer

*During that long period, the king of Egypt died. The Israelites groaned in their slavery and cried out, and their cry for help because of their slavery went up to God. God heard their groaning and he remembered his covenant with Abraham, with Isaac and with Jacob. So God looked on the Israelites and was concerned about them.*

Exodus 2:23-25

"**Y**ou sound bitter." Words spoken from my mom gave me alarm, because I knew they were true. I knew what that meant. Over the years, unforgiveness had been such a stronghold to overcome. This time I found myself still harboring resentment over the recent disappointment of others. Though I had every right to be hurt, the constant mental replay of what happened only encouraged those feelings to remain. I wanted to let go and overcome. However, I was more invested in hanging onto my feelings than fighting for my freedom. The silent expectation to receive apologies and some type of explanation grew as days and months went by. Anger and hurt evolved into bitterness, because I failed to play a pivotal role in the story: Making the choice to place my hurt and key players in His hands. Everybody has a story. At one time or another, we've all experienced some form of despair, unforgiveness, loss—you name it.

For some, the task of 'getting over it' becomes too much to fathom, causing many to find comfort in their pain or facing the fear of letting go. The journey to get to the other side of freedom, joy, and contentment appears less likely to happen than hoped. Years down the road, many still find themselves having difficulty releasing whatever they're holding onto.

Do you want to made whole? The man at the pool of Bethesda was asked this question as he laid there sick for thirty-eight years (John 5:1-8). And this question is still asked of us today. That man's immediate response and excuse, indicated he needed more than a physical healing; what he needed was a change of heart. And we need one as well.

Remaining to be helped by others was his reasons for not being healed. If we choose to sit or remain in our sins and bondage because others are not responsive to our needs, *we* have hindered our own growth.

There is only One who can truly help and give us the deliverance that's desperately needed. God is concerned about our well-being and does not want us to be passive in developing mentally or spiritually. Whether your miracle happens suddenly or over time, partner with God to make the *choice*, shake off pride, and watch God deliver. He can work miracles on your behalf.

## Prayer

*Dear Lord, Thank you for your delivering power. I admit that although I want to be free, my pain has somehow been comforting in ways I can't explain. Only you can help and deliver me to freedom. I want to be free in Christ and grow forward. I'm tired of remaining in my sin or bondage. Please help me change my heart and be healed, so that I can serve you to the fullest and help others in need. Amen.*

## DAY THIRTY-SEVEN REFLECTIONS

## DAY THIRTY-SEVEN REFLECTIONS

# DAY 38

# Your Way of Escape

*No temptation has overtaken you except what is common to mankind. And God is faithful; he will not let you be tempted beyond what you can bear. But when you are tempted, he will also provide a way out so that you can endure it.*

1 Corinthians 10:13

Temptation does not discriminate. It preys on the young, old, rich and poor alike. With an ultimate plan to get you off track and destroy your witness, its ways are often subtle. While the spirit of man is strong, the flesh is certainly weak. Our human desires can entangle and cause us to doubt our beliefs, deliverance, and relationship with God. As if waiting on God wasn't challenging enough, a daily struggle to maintain sexual purity may also hold its unique test. Joseph in the old testament gives us an example that our walk with Christ may be upright. However, temptation can find you at the most unlikely places. For Joseph, that was his place of employment, and from those who should have known better. After dodging many advances from Potiphars' wife, Joseph finally had to run from his temptress as though he was running for his life! His desire to remain obedient to Christ was priority.

In addition, Joseph did not want to sin against his own body! Here's a single, God-fearing man who knew where his allegiance was in speech and in action. Today, the desire to conform to societal norms is present like never before. God knows and understands that sexual desires may be hard for you to withstand.

He is the author of love and sex, within the bounds of marriage between a man and woman. Your sexual appetite is nothing new to Him, nor is it strange. The desire to give of oneself is natural. However, understanding *how* to control it before marriage is key.

Your key to withstanding is strategic: Prayer, boundary setting, and accountability will be your lifeline. You were not made to fight alone. God has already given you the keys to win. He's promised that no temptation will overcome you. He's given you a way out. Take it. One day at a time.

## Prayer

*Dear Lord, Thank you for creating love and the desire to express that love in your way. I want to wait for your chosen person in my life to express those desires, but it's difficult. Please help me to remain in your will and not sin against You or my body. Thank you being a way of escape. And I thank you for having control over the temptation that will come in my life. Give me the tools and help that I need to withstand. I can't do this alone and I know you don't expect me to. But with you Lord, I know that I can pass each test that comes my way. I give you all of me and look forward to love when the time is right. Amen.*

## DAY THIRTY-EIGHT REFLECTIONS

# DAY THIRTY-EIGHT REFLECTIONS

DAY 39

# Your Living Word

*For the word of God is alive and powerful. It is sharper than the sharpest two-edged sword, cutting between soul and spirit between joint and marrow. It exposes our innermost thoughts and desires.*

Hebrews 4:12

"Dionnea, Everything you need is in the Word of God." Though our relationship didn't last, words spoken from an ex still stand as truth today. It began more than two thousand years ago, and to this day its popularity supersedes that of any other book. The Bible still remains the number one book sold and distributed in the world, and one whose author is still alive. No other book can live up to the standard of one hundred percent guarantee like the Word of God. In addition, none can be so life changing than the Bible, which shows us who we really are. One of my favorite movies, *The Book of Eli*, gives us a glimpse of just how powerful the Word of God is. With the book on his mind, the antagonist seeks to hunt others down to find the one thing that contained all the power. Why? Because *he* wanted power. This man who represented the opposite of good desired to have the Word of God. Not to be good, but with the intent to control others.

All throughout Joseph's life, he didn't have a Bible to guide or comfort him in his disappointments. Instead, Joseph had the voice and Spirit of God to walk with him. While you're going through moments of trials and frustrations, the word of God can provide guidance, teaching you how to handle any situation.

What I've found in my own life is that we can have the Word, but failing to take the time to *read* the Word hinders our growth as well. As life would have it, God would show me that failure to spend quality time in His word would leave me feeling depleted.

Going about my day, I was aware of the emptiness I felt. Not being able to pinpoint how and where, I asked God to show me what to do. The discovery that my emptiness stemmed from failing to study scripture was revealed. I knew that if growth and application was my goal, I needed to do better than before. Many seek change but fail at consistency in doing so. God doesn't want anyone to go through life without a guide.

This great book can impact, encourage, and transform your life from the inside out. When you purpose your heart to richly engage in God's Word consistently, He will show and teach you His ways, guaranteeing that your life will never be the same.

## Prayer

*Dear Lord, Thank you for your living Word. It has given me peace, comfort, and joy. Because I have your Word, I'm able to see how I can grow, stand against spiritual attacks, and have the joy that you freely give. Please forgive me for not spending as much time in your Word as I should. Please help me desire more of your Word in my life and illuminate my understanding. Amen.*

## DAY THIRTY-NINE REFLECTIONS

## DAY THIRTY-NINE REFLECTIONS

DAY 40

# Your Everything

*I am my beloved's, and my beloved is mine.*

Song of Solomon 6:3 (ESV)

"To have and to hold, from this day forward till death us do part." Words shared through generations have stood the test of time and, unfortunately, longer than some marriages. While attending weddings, I've often wondered if couples truly know the impact of their vows. It's no wonder that movies about love have romanticized weddings and marriage to a fault, where unrealistic themes and ideas have clouded the minds of many. Sadly, I was among those whose fantasy about love and the big day sometimes overrode moments of common sense and being spiritually led. Wanting someone to call my own, the desire to be chosen and validated resulted in foolishness and unrequited love. But one day, a wonderful change happened. Epiphany is what I like to call it. A moment when you realize the very thing your heart has desired had been with you all along—*everything* changes. The search for a soul mate or "the one" has left many empty handed and confused on the road to love. There is no shame in wanting to give of yourself completely.

However, having a God-given perspective in your desire and search makes all the difference. The marriage relationship originated by God represents a reflection of His love toward us. Vulnerability, care, and expression of love are the hallmarks of giving yourself unreservedly to someone.

Because God is so invested in His love for you, anything less than *His* best won't do. Whether stated or written on your heart, God understands the desire for wedded bliss.

There's no other person but God who can anticipate your wants, or know what you'll say before you say it. He will continue to love and pursue you in spite of flaws and failures. The infamous line, 'you complete me' should only be reserved for God. After all, He is the only One who has the power to transform us.

A love that's trusting and eternal. He is the only One who can meet your needs. It's because of the cross; *you* are already complete in Christ.

## Prayer

*Dear Lord, Thank you for being my everything and making my life complete. You continue to show me that I'm so loved by you and that I don't have to seek validation from others. You keep your promises and satisfy my soul with your love. No matter what season I find myself in, I know that you are there with me. Thank you Lord, for saying, "no" and "wait," so that I can draw closer to you. Thank you for these sacred moments in the middle. I am forever yours. Amen.*

## DAY FORTY REFLECTIONS

## DAY FORTY REFLECTIONS

## A Final Word

There will be no other time than your single season to fully divert your attention and develop an awesome relationship with God. Funny how time and a change in perspective, can make you appreciate what you considered to be a nuisance at one time. In the past, I found a common Bible verse used to encourage singles to be anything but: *I want you to be free from the concerns of this life. An unmarried man can spend his time doing the Lord's work and thinking how to please him (1 Corinthians 7:32, NLT).* However, I'm now thankful for my season and development as a woman of God during these moments of growth.

If someone would have told *me* at twenty-five that I would write a book on encouraging other singles in their journey, I'm sure laughter would have been my first response.

I understand now. I understand the hardship, quiet moments, and triumphs have not only laid the foundation for marriage. But, it's also prepared me to become more empathetic to others in whatever state they find themselves in.

During this time, allow God to do a work in you. Allow God to love you and dismantle wrong thinking, behavior, and attitudes that can hinder your growth as a Christian and spouse. After all, at the end of the day, it's really all about Him! Let God transform your life, so that you can be prepared to handle your next place of promise. The tools you gain in these moments, will be needed in your next season.

As I was in the midst of finishing this book, thoughts of offense came to mind and I almost began to entertain them with feelings of anger and hurt. However, a gentle reminder from the Holy Spirit stopped me in my tracks. Quickly, words written in this devotional to help *you* came to mind.

It's amazing how the Holy Spirit will cause things to come back to your remembrance. Don't be surprised if God does the very same thing with you. As you are encouraged, don't neglect to pass it on. I'm sure someone needs what you've been imparted with.

Life is made to be enjoyed. Therefore, enjoy your life- challenges and all, trust God, and don't waste the wait!

### Ecclesiastes 3:1, NLT

**For everything there is a season, a time for every activity under heaven.**

Direct all correspondence and inquiries to:

**A Single Moment**

**Encouraging Hearts, Inspiring Minds**

www.a-single-moment.com

asinglemoment1@gmail.com

Connect with Dionnea Seals on social media

Facebook: asinglemomentd

Twitter: asinglemoment1

www.ingramcontent.com/pod-product-compliance
Lightning Source LLC
LaVergne TN
LVHW041248080426
835510LV00009B/642